100 Days of Mindfulness:
PRESENCE

100 Days of Mindfulness:
PRESENCE

A Journal

Tracey Moore Lukkarila

Yesterday is already gone.
Tomorrow is not yet here.
Today is the only day available to us.
It is the most important day of our lives.

--Thich Nhat Hanh, "Moments of Mindfulness"

Contents

Preface

On my journey of dealing with clinical depression,
I've tried many things. One thing that's remained a constant
is journaling. I find journaling keeps me on point and
accountable to whatever therapeutic treatment I'm
undertaking at the time. Sometimes I journal a lot of words,
but most of time it's a simple daily check-in.

For the past two years, my journal has been focused on
mindfulness. I have collected dozens of mindfulness activities
from my readings and trainings, modifying many of them to
be more meaningful to me. These activities have had a
profound impact on my depression and have been literally
lifesaving.

I started to realize I had the foundation of a journal I could
share with others. The format of this journal mirrors my own
handwritten journal. Each day I record what I'm grateful for,
what I did successfully that day, and what's on my mind,
such as my experience with whatever mindfulness
technique(s) I did that day.

I hope you find this journal as helpful as I have.

--Tracey Moore Lukkarila, June 2016

Acknowledgments

In 2014, I read two books that radically changed how I had been dealing with my depression, putting me on a path of mindfulness: "The Happiness Trap" by Russ Harris, PhD, and "Authentic Happiness" by Martin Seligman, PhD. For two decades, therapists had focused on digging deep to find the root of my depression, giving importance and meaning to my obsessive thoughts. I thought they were a reflection of who I am. It was a revelation to learn that thoughts are incredibly random and I can choose what I do with them. I don't have to analyze them or identify with them if I don't want to, and I certainly don't have to follow their lead. I began to see a way to loosen the grip of obsessive thoughts that kept me so preoccupied I was missing out on life.

Since then, I've become something of a mindfulness collector. The mindfulness activities in this journal are an amalgamation of techniques I've learned from others and found useful. I thank Russ Harris, PhD; Martin Seligman, PhD; Elisha Goldstein, PhD; Bob Stahl, PhD; Baron Baptiste; Brene Brown, PhD; Jon and Leah Hanson; Danielle Schellhorn; Karina Hahn; Rebecca Farinas, MD; the Wekiva Springs therapy team; the teachers at the Amrit Yoga Institute; Cindy Richetti, LMHC; and Lynn Powell, LMHC.

Turning my messy handwritten journal into a book was work (to say the least)! I honor and very much appreciate my companions on this journey. Katherine Bates patiently read through both the printed and eBook versions, tidying up my grammar. My husband Troy Lukkarila gave me new ideas for improving my collection of mindfulness techniques, enriching my experience (and hopefully yours) with these exercises. Finally, Lisa Spirko edited for consistent formatting and wording, removing so many unnecessary words I lost count! Thank you so much for your sharp eye and beautiful ability to boil down the English language to its essence. You are an amazing editor.

Introduction

What exactly is mindfulness? Simply stated, it's the practice of living in the moment. Sounds easy enough, but it's actually really hard. Our brains are wired to think, think, think all the time. Whether we're thinking about something that happened a year ago or an hour ago, our thoughts take us away from focusing on right here, right now.

This constant mental chatter can be annoying and tiring. But it can also have serious consequences in our lives. In my case, this habit of constantly thinking and ruminating fed my clinical depression and turned it into obsessive-compulsive disorder. The inability to quiet my mind literally drove me crazy, leading to 13 days in a mental health facility.

> When we spend so much time in our heads, we take ourselves out of the only time we really have, which is now. Our runaway minds rob us of our very lives.

Staying healthy and helping others is my passion. I've had thousands of hours of professional therapy, read numerous self-help books, taken dozens of workshops, and even became a yoga instructor. Through all of this, mindfulness is the tool I use every day. It calms my mind, helping me to be more at peace with my depression. Best of all, mindfulness has shortened my depressive episodes so I get past them and back into my life sooner.

I think the beauty of this journal is that it's actually my journal. I am not a therapist. I am simply a patient sharing something that personally works for me.

Some of the exercises in the journal will seem simplistic. If you're like me, you will wonder what purpose they serve. I totally get it. If I hadn't taken a chance and tried these exercises myself, I would have missed out on something that really helps. When you feel like quitting, remember that you are working a new muscle in your brain, and just like physical exercise, training the mind takes time. I encourage you to hang in there and see what happens. Expect to spend 15-20 minutes a day.

Mindfulness exercises are designed to shift your focus to something happening right now, providing a short-circuit to negative thinking. Don't be fooled by their simplicity though. They really work! Practicing them over time has made it possible for me to shift my obsessive thinking and anxiety to calm presence whenever I want. Other things have improved in my life as well:

- My experience of life is better. My runaway thoughts would get in the way of everything. Now I catch myself a lot sooner and have simple tools to bring myself out of my head.

- I love my husband more. Isn't that crazy? But it's true! Mindfulness has improved my ability to focus on what he's saying and not get caught up in my thoughts. When I'm with him, I'm able to really experience being with him. I feel a lot more connected to him.

- My relationships are richer. I feel more connected with family and friends too.

- I can focus in business meetings. I used to have a terrible time staying tuned in when people talked. Now I use mindfulness to calm my thoughts and maintain my focus.

> I used to think the goal of mindfulness is to control our thoughts. But our practice is to shift our focus and let our thoughts fade into the background. Let them decrease in volume so they stop stealing the show.

- I'm much more grateful. I have more appreciation for the people in my life and the abundance I have. I am more aware of things I used to overlook.

- I'm a safer driver. Because I've learned how to stay focused, I am less distracted.

My sincere hope is this journal will help you on your path to living more fully in the present. It's time to get out of your head and into your life!

Day 1: 1-11-19

Reframe One Negative Thought You Had Today

Reframing negative thoughts trains your brain to consider more positive, reasonable alternatives. Because negative thoughts take us out of the present moment and into our heads, practicing reframing helps you to move past the thoughts quicker so you can return to the present.

Give it a try! Reword a negative thought into a positive/rational one.

Negative Thought	Positive/Rational Alternative
Example:	Example:
I never do anything right.	*Perfection is an unrealistic goal.*
I can't do it.	w/God anything is possible
I'm fat	I'm fearfully & wonderfully made

Easy does it. Don't worry about doing any of this "right." If you can't fill in all the blanks, who cares? This is your journey. You're just getting started. Take it slow.

Gratitude List

It's natural for our brains to be overrun with judgment, negativity, worries. Developing a gratitude attitude trains your brain to focus less on the negative and more on the positive. It trains you to consider things you overlook and take for granted. Focusing on little things is where the magic of mindfulness lives.

> Don't know where to start? Here are some things to be grateful for: clean running water, roof over your head, air conditioning, clean air to breathe.

Try it! List 5 things you are grateful for.

- My education
- clean water
- my family
- Lily
- my friendships

Successes

Patting yourself on the back for the things you do each day, big and small, brings greater awareness to yourself and your impact in the world.

Try it! List 3 things you did well today.

- _____
- _____
- _____

> Don't discount the power of small successes. Sometimes just getting out of bed is an achievement! Celebrate your little successes too!

Day 2: March 26, 2020

Reframe One Negative Thought You Had Today
Reword a negative thought into a positive or rational one.

Negative Thought
Example:
(I am a failure.)

Positive/Rational Alternative
Example:
*I am a hard-working person striving
to learn from my mistakes*

_____   _____

_____   _____

_____   _____

_____   _____

_____   _____

_____   _____

Gratitude List
List 5 things you are
grateful for.

> More ideas: having a wide variety
> of foods available, amazing
> movies/TV shows to watch, car or
> transportation.

- ❧ _____
- ❧ _____
- ❧ _____
- ❧ _____
- ❧ _____

Successes
Pat yourself on the back for 3
things you did well today.

> Being able to focus and really
> enjoy a meal is a success. So is
> taking care of your teeth.

- ❧ _____
- ❧ _____
- ❧ _____

Reframe One Negative Thought You Had Today
Reword a negative thought into a positive or rational one.

Negative Thought
Example:
I can't stop feeling scared.

Positive/Rational Alternative
Example:
I am a courageous person working on facing my fears.

I'm scared to interview.   I am courageous and qualified.
I'm fat.   I am made in his image. teach

Gratitude List
List 5 things you are grateful for.

Name a person you love, or someone who inspired you or helped you.

- My health (covid-19)
- Austin - his calm personality
- Bethany - a good person to quarantine with
- Food - not everyone can buy in bulk
- My mom - making sure I'm ok and mentally healthy

Successes
Pat yourself on the back for 3 things you did well today.

Being in the moment and feeling fun and joy is a success. Recount fun things you did.

- I worked out.
- I took Lily on a walk.
- I cleaned!

Day 4: _____

Reframe One Negative Thought You Had Today
Reword a negative thought into a positive or rational one.

Negative Thought
Example:
I'll never get better.

Positive/Rational Alternative
Example:
I make progress every day. I am allowing my illness to teach me more about myself.

_____   _____

_____   _____

_____   _____

_____   _____

_____   _____

Gratitude List
List 5 things you are grateful for.

Having food and being able to taste it is a gift.

- _____
- _____
- _____
- _____
- _____

Successes
Pat yourself on the back for 3 things you did well today.

Mundane things like cooking and cleaning are successes too, particularly when you are ill, sad, or tired.

- _____
- _____
- _____

Great Job!

Now that you've practiced the foundation of the journal,
we'll add a mindfulness exercise every few days.
Below is the first one.

Approach these mindfulness exercises with as much ease as
possible. Do not struggle with them. There is no perfect way
to do them. Let yourself be messy.

Enjoy the journey.

First Mindfulness Assignment:
Sense of Smell

At least once a day, take five minutes to tune into
your sense of smell. Set your timer so you ensure
you use the full five minutes. Take deep breaths
and concentrate on fragrances around you. If your
mind starts to wander, gently bring your attention
back to your sense of smell. If your mind wanders
again, just calmly return to smell. It's okay if you
have to do this several times. That's just part of
the practice.

Day 5: _____

Reframe One Negative Thought You Had Today
Reword a negative thought into a positive or rational one.

Negative Thought	**Positive/Rational Alternative**
_____	_____
_____	_____
_____	_____
_____	_____
_____	_____
_____	_____

Gratitude List
List 5 things you are grateful for.

- ❧ _____
- ❧ _____
- ❧ _____
- ❧ _____
- ❧ _____

> Having a home to live in, bed to
> sleep in, kitchen to cook in – all
> things to be grateful for.

Successes
Pat yourself on the back for 3 things you did well today.

- ❧ _____
- ❧ _____
- ❧ _____

> Having the ability to truly
> enjoy yourself is a success.

Mindfulness Assignment: Sense of Smell

Write about your experience with the mindfulness exercise. What did you notice? How did the smells register in your body? Did your mind wander off? Were you able to bring your focus back to your sense of smell? What thoughts did you have? If you didn't do the assignment, what got in the way?

One definition of mindfulness: *Paying attention on purpose and without judgment.*

–Drs. Elisha Goldstein and Bob Stahl, "MBSR Every Day: Daily Practices from the Heart of Mindfulness-Based Stress Reduction"

Day 6: _____

Reframing Negative Thoughts

Now that you've done this activity for a few days, you
know how to reframe negative thoughts. Try doing this on the fly as
negative thoughts occur throughout the day. We won't journal this
going forward. Periodically I will remind you to incorporate this as
a daily habit.

Gratitude List

List 5 things you are grateful for.

- _____
- _____
- _____
- _____
- _____

Successes

Pat yourself on the back for 3 things you did well today.

- _____
- _____
- _____

Mindfulness Assignment: Sense of Smell

Write about your experiences.

_____

_____

_____

_____

_____

_____

_____

_____

_____

_____

_____

_____

_____

Day 7:

Gratitude List
List 5 things you are grateful for.

🙎 _____

🙎 _____

🙎 _____

🙎 _____

🙎 _____

Successes
List 3 things you did well today.

🙎 _____

🙎 _____

🙎 _____

Mindfulness Assignment: Sense of Smell
How did the mindfulness assignment go? What did you notice?

_____

_____

_____

_____

_____

_____

_____

> *One of the wonderful things about mindfulness is that it encourages us to break out of routine and fall back into the wonder of daily life.*
>
> —Drs. Elisha Goldstein and Bob Stahl, "MBSR Every Day: Daily Practices from the Heart of Mindfulness-Based Stress Reduction"

_____

_____

_____

Day 8: _____

Gratitude List
List 5 things you are grateful for.

- _____
- _____
- _____
- _____
- _____

Successes
List 3 things you did well today.

- _____
- _____
- _____

Mindfulness Assignment: Sense of Smell
How did the mindfulness assignment go? What did you notice?

_____

_____

_____

_____

_____

_____

_____

_____

Next Mindfulness Assignment:
Clean Water
For the next few days, whenever you fill a glass
or container with water, think of how grateful
you are to have clean running water. Really take
time to ponder this. If your mind wanders, gently
return your focus to the water.

Thank you Leah Hansen, co-owner of Hot Spot Power Yoga in
Jacksonville, FL, for giving me this idea.

Day 9:

Gratitude List
List 5 things you are grateful for.

- _____
- _____
- _____
- _____
- _____

Successes
List 3 things you did well today.

- _____
- _____
- _____

Mindfulness Assignment: Clean Water
How did the mindfulness assignment go? What did you experience?
If you forgot, what got in the way? Are you beating yourself up
now for forgetting? (Don't!)

_____
_____
_____
_____
_____
_____
_____
_____
_____
_____
_____
_____
_____
_____
_____
_____

Day 10: _____

Gratitude List
List 5 things you are grateful for.

- _____
- _____
- _____
- _____
- _____

Successes
List 3 things you did well today.

- _____
- _____
- _____

Mindfulness Assignment: Clean Water
Write about your experiences.

_____

_____

_____

_____

_____

_____

_____

_____

_____

_____

_____

_____

_____

_____

_____

_____

Gratitude works! In 2003, two researchers studied three groups of people. One group counted five blessings per day, one group counted five burdens per day, and one group wrote about neutral events. The blessings group experienced significantly less stress and more well-being.

–Drs. Elisha Goldstein and Bob Stahl, "MBSR Every Day: Daily Practices from the Heart of Mindfulness-Based Stress Reduction"

Day 11:

Gratitude List
List 5 things you are grateful for.

- _____
- _____
- _____
- _____
- _____

Successes
List 3 things you did well today.

- _____
- _____
- _____

Mindfulness Assignment: Clean Water
Write about your experiences.

_____

_____

_____

_____

_____

_____

_____

Next Mindfulness Assignment:
Fingertip Focus

Every day, sit in a quiet spot. Put your hands together
with fingertips touching. Close your eyes or set your
gaze softly on one spot in front of you. Breathe
deeply and bring your attention to each finger
individually, one-by-one. Be grateful for your hands.
Keep breathing and focusing for two minutes. If your
mind wanders, gently return to your fingers.

Thank you Jon Hansen, co-owner of Hot Spot Power Yoga in Jacksonville,
FL, for giving me this idea.

Day 12: _____

Gratitude List
List 5 things you are grateful for.

- _____
- _____
- _____
- _____
- _____

Successes
List 3 things you did well today.

- _____
- _____
- _____

Mindfulness Assignment: Fingertip Focus

How did the assignment go? What did you experience as you focused on each fingertip one-by-one? Did giving thanks to your hands change your perspective? Were you able to get out of your head and really focus on your fingers?

_____

_____

_____

_____

_____

_____

_____

_____

_____

_____

_____

_____

_____

Day 13:

Gratitude List
List 5 things you are grateful for.

- ❧ _____
- ❧ _____
- ❧ _____
- ❧ _____
- ❧ _____

Successes
List 3 things you did well today.

- ❧ _____
- ❧ _____
- ❧ _____

Mindfulness Assignment: Fingertip Focus
Write about your experiences.

_____

_____

_____

_____

_____

_____

_____

_____

_____

_____

_____

_____

_____

_____

_____

_____

_____

Day 14: _____

Gratitude List
List 5 things you are grateful for.

- ꙮ _____
- ꙮ _____
- ꙮ _____
- ꙮ _____
- ꙮ _____

Successes
List 3 things you did well today.

- ꙮ _____
- ꙮ _____
- ꙮ _____

Mindfulness Assignment: Fingertip Focus
Write about your experiences.

_____

_____

_____

_____

_____

_____

_____

_____

_____

_____

_____

_____

_____

> As you complete your gratitude and successes each day, try not to be repetitive. It's easy to fall into a rut of repeating the same things over and over in your journal. Challenge yourself to think differently. Even if it's the same thought, reword it so it has a slightly different meaning. See the appendix for ways I've done this.

Day 15: _____

Gratitude List
List 5 things you are grateful for.

- _____
- _____
- _____
- _____
- _____

Successes
List 3 things you did well today.

- _____
- _____
- _____

Mindfulness Assignment: Fingertip Focus
Write about your experiences.

_____

_____

_____

_____

We don't stop playing because we grow old. We grow old because we stop playing.

—George Bernard Shaw

_____

_____

_____

_____

_____

_____

_____

Day 16: _____

Gratitude List
List 5 things you are grateful for.

- ê _____
- ê _____
- ê _____
- ê _____
- ê _____

Successes
List 3 things you did well today.

- ê _____
- ê _____
- ê _____

Mindfulness Assignment: Fingertip Focus
Write about your experiences.

_____

_____

_____

_____

_____

_____

_____

_____

_____

_____

Next Mindfulness Assignment:
Eating with Intention
Be mindful during one meal a day. Eat in a quiet
environment (no TV, computer, or other distractions.)
Notice the aromas, feel the texture of the food, chew
slowly and focus on how the flavor changes.

Day 17:

Gratitude List
List 5 things you are grateful for.

- _____
- _____
- _____
- _____
- _____

Successes
List 3 things you did well today.

- _____
- _____
- _____

Mindfulness Assignment: Eating with Intention
How did eating mindfully go today? What smells, textures, and flavors did you notice? What was it like eating in a quiet environment, really focusing on your food?

_____

_____

_____

_____

_____

_____

_____

_____

_____

_____

_____

_____

_____

_____

Day 18: _____

Gratitude List
List 5 things you are grateful for.

- _____
- _____
- _____
- _____
- _____

Successes
List 3 things you did well today.

- _____
- _____
- _____

Mindfulness Assignment: Eating with Intention
Write about your experiences.

_____

_____

_____

_____

_____

_____

_____

_____

_____

_____

_____

_____

_____

_____

_____

_____

_____

_____

_____

Day 19:

Gratitude List
List 5 things you are grateful for.

-
-
-
-
-

Successes
List 3 things you did well today.

-
-
-

Mindfulness Assignment: Eating with Intention
Write about your experiences.

Reframing reminder:
Are you still using the mental practice of reframing to consider alternatives to negative thoughts that come to you throughout the day?

You can use reframing in your eating assignment. Maybe you have foods you don't like, or worry will make you gain weight. Can you see the food a different way?

Day 20:

Gratitude List
List 5 things you are grateful for.

- ✍ _____
- ✍ _____
- ✍ _____
- ✍ _____
- ✍ _____

> Name a person. Write down one thing you like about them. Repeat daily until you run out of ideas. You may find you appreciate far more about them than you realize.

Successes
List 3 things you did well today.

- ✍ _____
- ✍ _____
- ✍ _____

Mindfulness Assignment: Eating with Intention
Write about your experiences.

_____

_____

_____

_____

_____

_____

_____

_____

_____

_____

_____

_____

_____

_____

Each bite of food contains the life of the Sun and the Earth. The whole universe is in a piece of bread.

–Thich Nhat Hanh, "Moments of Mindfulness"

Day 21:

Gratitude List
List 5 things you are grateful for.

- _____
- _____
- _____
- _____
- _____

Successes
List 3 things you did well today.

- _____
- _____
- _____

Mindfulness Assignment: Eating with Intention
Write about your experiences.

_____

_____

_____

_____

_____

_____

_____

_____

_____

Next Mindfulness Assignment:
Dishwashing
As you wash dishes, think about how grateful you
are that you have clean running water. Focus on
how the water and the suds feel on your hands.
Notice the dishes you have. Mentally give thanks
for what you have.

Thank you Leah Hansen, co-owner of Hot Spot Power Yoga in
Jacksonville FL for giving me this idea.

Day 22:

Gratitude List
List 5 things you are grateful for.

- ❧ _____
- ❧ _____
- ❧ _____
- ❧ _____
- ❧ _____

Successes
List 3 things you did well today.

- ❧ _____
- ❧ _____
- ❧ _____

Mindfulness Assignment: Dishwashing
How did your mindfulness assignment go? Did you notice how clean the water is, and give thanks? What was it like washing dishes with intention and gratitude?

_____

_____

_____

_____

_____

_____

_____

_____

_____

_____

_____

_____

_____

_____

_____

_____

Day 23:

Gratitude List
List 5 things you are grateful for.

- ❧ _____
- ❧ _____
- ❧ _____
- ❧ _____
- ❧ _____

Successes
List 3 things you did well today.

- ❧ _____
- ❧ _____
- ❧ _____

Mindfulness Assignment: Dishwashing
Write about your experiences.

_____

_____

_____

_____

_____

_____

_____

_____

_____

_____

_____

_____

_____

_____

_____

_____

_____

When you are washing the dishes, washing the dishes must be the most important thing in your life. Just as when you're drinking tea, drinking tea must be the most important thing in your life...Each act must be carried out in mindfulness. Each act is a rite, a ceremony.

–Thich Nhat Hanh
From the book "The Pocket Therapist" by Therese Borchard

Day 24: _____

Gratitude List
List 5 things you are grateful for.

- _____
- _____
- _____
- _____
- _____

Successes
List 3 things you did well today.

- _____
- _____
- _____

Mindfulness Assignment: Dishwashing
Write about your experiences.

_____
_____
_____
_____
_____
_____
_____
_____
_____
_____
_____
_____
_____
_____
_____
_____
_____
_____
_____

Gratitude List
List 5 things you are grateful for.

- _____
- _____
- _____
- _____
- _____

Successes
List 3 things you did well today.

- _____
- _____
- _____

Mindfulness Assignment: Dishwashing
Write about your experiences.

_____
_____
_____
_____
_____
_____
_____
_____
_____
_____
_____
_____
_____
_____
_____
_____
_____

Mega Mindfulness Assignment:
Values-Based Living

Do you struggle with your job or other obligations? Do you find yourself unfulfilled and wishing for more? You can use reframing to see different ways to respond to situations, to shift your perspective and to bring awareness to what you really want in life.

Step 1: Write down 3 or 4 words to describe your values (e.g., compassion, generosity, truthfulness). Choose simple words you can easily recall during the day.

Step 2: As you move through your day, be mindful of your actions and reactions. Are you living your values, even in small ways? Or are you doing things that undermine them? What can you do to serve your values better?

As you actively shift your thinking and behaviors to align with your values, you'll find more satisfaction in your daily activities. You'll better see the connection between what's in your heart and what you express in the world, empowering you to make meaningful changes.

Remember: Values are different from goals. While goals describe milestones to achieve, values describe attitudes we hold dear. In the busyness of our lives, we often fail to notice when our actions veer away from our values.

Tip: The appendix has a list of values and additional guidance for this mega assignment.

Day 26:

Gratitude List
List 5 things you are grateful for.

- ❧ _____
- ❧ _____
- ❧ _____
- ❧ _____
- ❧ _____

Successes
List 3 things you did well today.

- ❧ _____
- ❧ _____
- ❧ _____

Mega Mindfulness Assignment: Value-Based Living
Write down your 3-4 values and examples of how you lived them
in the last 24 hours. Did you do anything that undermined them?
What are some ideas for better serving them next time?"

_____
_____
_____
_____
_____
_____
_____
_____
_____
_____
_____
_____
_____
_____
_____
_____

Day 27: _____

Gratitude List
List 5 things you are grateful for.

- ✍ _____
- ✍ _____
- ✍ _____
- ✍ _____
- ✍ _____

Catch the moment!
Be grateful for the people who support you. Tell them "thank you." Write about what they mean to you. Share your thoughts with them.

Successes
List 3 things you did well today.

- ✍ _____
- ✍ _____
- ✍ _____

Mega Mindfulness Assignment: Value-Based Living
Write about your experiences.

_____
_____
_____
_____
_____
_____
_____
_____
_____
_____
_____
_____
_____
_____
_____
_____
_____
_____
_____

Day 28: _____

Gratitude List
List 5 things you are grateful for.

- ✌ _____
- ✌ _____
- ✌ _____
- ✌ _____
- ✌ _____

Successes
List 3 things you did well today.

- ✌ _____
- ✌ _____
- ✌ _____

Mega Mindfulness Assignment: Value-Based Living
Write about your experiences.

_____

_____

_____

_____

_____

_____

_____

_____

_____

_____

_____

_____

_____

_____

_____

_____

_____

_____

...one of the final steps in healing our wounded inner child is learning how to stay with our loneliness; not running away from it or rushing into some activity as a kind of anesthesia. God, does that hurt; staying with the pain of unfulfilled love, expectations, and aspirations. And yet, letting the loneliness come and go as it wants, exactly how our neighborhood dog did when I was ten, is, I suspect, the single most liberating step in my recovery from depression and anxiety.

– Therese Borchard, "The Pocket Therapist"

_____

_____

Day 29: _____

Gratitude List
List 5 things you are grateful for.

- _____
- _____
- _____
- _____
- _____

Successes
List 3 things you did well today.

- _____
- _____
- _____

Mega Mindfulness Assignment: Value-Based Living
Write about your experiences.

_____

_____

_____

_____

_____

_____

_____

_____

_____

_____

_____

_____

_____

_____

_____

_____

_____

_____

_____

_____

_____

Day 30: _____

Gratitude List
List 5 things you are grateful for.

- _____
- _____
- _____
- _____
- _____

Successes
List 3 things you did well today.

> **This is day 30!** You've done this journal for 30 days! Celebrate that success!

- _____
- _____
- _____

Mega Mindfulness Assignment: Value-Based Living
Write about your experiences.

_____
_____
_____
_____
_____
_____
_____
_____

Next Mindfulness Assignment:
Silent Commuting
Turn your commute into a silent meditation. Drivers, roll up windows and turn off the stereo. Riders, use headphones to block out sounds (white noise/nature sounds work great.) No cell phone or electronics. Enjoy the quiet. Feel the steering wheel under your fingers, the seat under your hips, the pedals/floor under your feet. Notice the world through the windows. Breathe.

Day 31: _____

Gratitude List
List 5 things you are grateful for.

- _____
- _____
- _____
- _____
- _____

Successes
List 3 things you did well today.

- _____
- _____
- _____

Mindfulness Assignment: Silent Commuting
How was silent commuting? Did you notice your mind wandering?
Did you experience the whole trip, or were there parts you don't
recall? (You know how some days you go all the way to work or
home and don't remember anything about it?) What did you see
outside the window? What was it like to be more mindful?

_____

_____

_____

_____

_____

_____

_____

_____

_____

_____

_____

_____

_____

Day 32: _____

Gratitude List
List 5 things you are grateful for.

- _____
- _____
- _____
- _____
- _____

Successes
List 3 things you did well today.

- _____
- _____
- _____

Mindfulness Assignment: Silent Commuting
Write about your experiences.

_____
_____
_____
_____
_____
_____
_____
_____
_____
_____
_____
_____
_____
_____
_____
_____
_____
_____
_____
_____

Day 33: _____

Gratitude List
List 5 things you are grateful for.

- ❧ _____
- ❧ _____
- ❧ _____
- ❧ _____
- ❧ _____

Successes
List 3 things you did well today.

- ❧ _____
- ❧ _____
- ❧ _____

Mindfulness Assignment: Silent Commuting
Write about your experiences.

_____

_____

_____

_____

_____

_____

_____

_____

Catch the moment!
When someone says something funny, laugh heartily! Feel the laughter in your entire body. Just go with it! Don't get caught up in your thoughts or worry about what other people think.

_____

_____

Day 34: _____

Gratitude List
List 5 things you are grateful for.

- _____
- _____
- _____
- _____
- _____

Successes
List 3 things you did well today.

- _____
- _____
- _____

Mindfulness Assignment: Silent Commuting
Write about your experiences.

_____

_____

_____

_____

_____

_____

Next Mindfulness Assignment:
Bedtime
Each night when you lie down for bed, take at least 5 minutes to notice how good the bed feels. Lie on your back and notice how the mattress feels on your backside. Move your attention from feet to legs to buttocks, then back, shoulders, arms, neck, head. Then notice how the sheets feel on the front of your body, from feet to head. Give thanks for your bed.
~ extra assignment ~
Whenever you flush the toilet, think of how grateful you are to have plumbing.

Day 35: _____

Gratitude List
List 5 things you are grateful for.

♌ _____
♌ _____
♌ _____
♌ _____
♌ _____

Successes
List 3 things you did well today.

♌ _____
♌ _____
♌ _____

Mindfulness Assignment: Bedtime
How did the bedtime assignment go? What sensations did you
notice in your body? How did giving thanks for your bed change
your perception about your bedroom, sleeping, house, life
circumstance? Did you do the extra assignment to feel grateful for
plumbing? What did you notice in your attitude?

_____
_____
_____
_____
_____
_____
_____
_____
_____
_____
_____
_____
_____
_____

Day 36:

Gratitude List
List 5 things you are grateful for.

- ❧ _____
- ❧ _____
- ❧ _____
- ❧ _____
- ❧ _____

Successes
List 3 things you did well today.

- ❧ _____
- ❧ _____
- ❧ _____

Mindfulness Assignment: Bedtime
Write about your experiences.

_____

_____

_____

_____

_____

_____

_____

_____

_____

_____

_____

_____

_____

_____

_____

_____

_____

_____

Day 37: _____

Gratitude List
List 5 things you are grateful for.

- _____
- _____
- _____
- _____
- _____

Successes
List 3 things you did well today.

- _____
- _____
- _____

Mindfulness Assignment: Bedtime
Write about your experiences.

_____

_____

_____

_____

_____

_____

_____

_____

_____

_____

_____

Make a moment!
Spend time with a pet. Don't have a pet? Visit a local shelter or a friend who has a pet. Enjoy the feeling of petting an animal. Focus on its fur, the sounds it makes, the warmth of its body, it's response to your petting. Really be with the animal.

Day 38:

Gratitude List
List 5 things you are grateful for.

-
-
-
-
-

Successes
List 3 things you did well today.

-
-
-

Mindfulness Assignment: Bedtime
Write about your experiences.

_____

_____

_____

_____

_____

_____

_____

_____

_____

_____

Next Mindfulness Assignment:
Shower Sounds

As you shower this week, focus on sound. Listen to how the water pressure fluctuates, how it sounds hitting you vs. hitting the floor. Listen how shampooing, lathering, shaving, and rinsing all sound different.

Day 39: _____

Gratitude List
List 5 things you are grateful for.

- _____
- _____
- _____
- _____
- _____

Successes
List 3 things you did well today.

- _____
- _____
- _____

Mindfulness Assignment: Shower Sounds
What was it like to focus on sounds in the shower? Did you hear sounds you hadn't noticed before? Were you able to stay focused on the sounds or did your mind wander? What was that like?

_____
_____
_____
_____
_____
_____
_____
_____
_____
_____
_____
_____
_____
_____
_____
_____

Day 40:

Gratitude List
List 5 things you are grateful for.

-
-
-
-
-

Successes
List 3 things you did well today.

-
-
-

Mindfulness Assignment: Shower Sounds
Write about your experiences.

_____

_____

_____

_____

_____

_____

_____

_____

_____

_____

_____

_____

_____

_____

_____

_____

_____

_____

Day 41: _____

Gratitude List
List 5 things you are grateful for.

- ❧ _____
- ❧ _____
- ❧ _____
- ❧ _____
- ❧ _____

Successes
List 3 things you did well today.

- ❧ _____
- ❧ _____
- ❧ _____

Mindfulness Assignment: Shower Sounds
Write about your experiences.

_____

_____

_____

_____

_____

_____

_____

_____

_____

_____

_____

_____

_____

_____

_____

_____

_____

Day 42:

Gratitude List
List 5 things you are grateful for.

- ❧ _____
- ❧ _____
- ❧ _____
- ❧ _____
- ❧ _____

Successes
List 3 things you did well today.

- ❧ _____
- ❧ _____
- ❧ _____

Mindfulness Assignment: Shower Sounds
Write about your experiences.

_____

_____

_____

_____

_____

_____

_____

_____

_____

Next Mindfulness Assignment:
Courtesy to Others
Each day, acknowledge wait staff, cashiers, and other
service people you encounter. Set down your phone and
give them your full attention. Look them in the eyes.
Smile warmly, even if you don't feel like it. Be thankful
for them. Tell them you appreciate them.

Thank you Brene Brown, PhD, author of many books such as "Daring Greatly,"
for giving me this idea. Check her out on **YouTube**.

Day 43: _____

Gratitude List
List 5 things you are grateful for.

- _____
- _____
- _____
- _____
- _____

Successes
List 3 things you did well today.

- _____
- _____
- _____

Mindfulness Assignment: Courtesy to Others
What was it like to show more courtesy to service people? Were you able to put down your phone and give them your full attention? Did this help you feel present and connected? What positive or negative feelings came up?

_____

_____

_____

_____

_____

_____

_____

_____

_____

_____

_____

_____

_____

_____

_____

Day 44:

Gratitude List
List 5 things you are grateful for.

-
-
-
-
-

Successes
List 3 things you did well today.

-
-
-

Mindfulness Assignment: Courtesy to Others
Write about your experiences.

People are illogical, unreasonable, and self-centered. Love them anyway.

– Kent Keith,
From the book "The Pocket Therapist" by Therese Borchard

Consider this is true for yourself as well – love yourself anyway!

Day 45: _____

Gratitude List
List 5 things you are grateful for.

- _____
- _____
- _____
- _____
- _____

Successes
List 3 things you did well today.

- _____
- _____
- _____

Mindfulness Assignment: Courtesy to Others
Write about your experiences.

_____

_____

_____

_____

_____

_____

_____

_____

_____

_____

_____

Reframing reminder:
How are you doing with mentally of reframing your negative thoughts? This can help you when dealing with the strangers. Rather than judging, consider you know nothing this person and their life. Can you acknowledge them with compassion instead?

Day 46:

Gratitude List
List 5 things you are grateful for.

- _____
- _____
- _____
- _____
- _____

Successes
List 3 things you did well today.

- _____
- _____
- _____

Mindfulness Assignment: Courtesy to Others
Write about your experiences.

_____

_____

_____

_____

_____

_____

_____

_____

_____

_____

_____

_____

Next Mindfulness Assignment:
Quiet Time
Every day, take five minutes to sit in complete silence.
Notice the subtle sounds. Feel the air on your skin.
Notice what your mind does in the quiet.

Day 47: _____

Gratitude List
List 5 things you are grateful for.

- _____
- _____
- _____
- _____
- _____

Successes
List 3 things you did well today.

- _____
- _____
- _____

Mindfulness Assignment: Quiet Time
What did you notice around you? What did your mind do in the quiet?

_____

_____

_____

_____

_____

_____

_____

_____

_____

_____

_____

_____

_____

_____

_____

_____

_____

_____

Day 48:

Gratitude List
List 5 things you are grateful for.

- ❧ _____
- ❧ _____
- ❧ _____
- ❧ _____
- ❧ _____

Successes
List 3 things you did well today.

- ❧ _____
- ❧ _____
- ❧ _____

Mindfulness Assignment: Quiet Time
Write about your experiences.

_____

_____

_____

_____

_____

_____

_____

_____

_____

_____

_____

_____

_____

_____

_____

_____

_____

_____

Day 49: _____

Gratitude List
List 5 things you are grateful for.

-   _____
-   _____
-   _____
-   _____
-   _____

Successes
List 3 things you did well today.

-   _____
-   _____
-   _____

Mindfulness Assignment: Quiet Time
Write about your experiences.

_____

_____

_____

_____

_____

_____

_____

_____

_____

_____

_____

_____

_____

Catch the moment!
When a friend invites you somewhere, GO! Don't let all the things you "should" do stop you. When you're with your friend, be present. Try not to be distracted, but instead be in the moment.

Day 50:

Gratitude List
List 5 things you are grateful for.

 _____
 _____
 _____
 _____
 _____

Successes
List 3 things you did well today.

_____
_____
_____

Mindfulness Assignment: Quiet Time
Write about your experiences.

_____
_____
_____
_____
_____
_____
_____
_____
_____
_____
_____
_____
_____
_____
_____
_____
_____
_____
_____

Day 51: _____

Gratitude List
List 5 things you are grateful for.

- _____
- _____
- _____
- _____
- _____

Successes
List 3 things you did well today.

- _____
- _____
- _____

Mindfulness Assignment: Quiet Time
Write about your experiences.

_____

_____

_____

_____

_____

_____

_____

_____

Next Mindfulness Assignment:
Good Hugs

Every day, give someone a big hug. Focus on how it feels. Don't get caught up in thoughts and judgments about the hug, just simply enjoy and feel it.

~ extra assignment ~

As people speak, resist the urge to interrupt or mentally rehearse what you're going to say. Instead, let them speak and focus on what they're saying.

Day 52: _____

Gratitude List
List 5 things you are grateful for.

- _____
- _____
- _____
- _____
- _____

Successes
List 3 things you did well today.

- _____
- _____
- _____

Mindfulness Assignment: Good Hugs
Did you mindfully hug someone today? Did anything in your mind stop you from fully enjoying the hug? Could you put the thoughts aside and refocus on the hug? Did you do the extra assignment of listening fully? Could you stay out of your head and really listen?

_____

_____

_____

_____

_____

_____

_____

_____

_____

_____

_____

_____

_____

_____

_____

Day 53: _____

Gratitude List
List 5 things you are grateful for.

- ✍ _____
- ✍ _____
- ✍ _____
- ✍ _____
- ✍ _____

Successes
List 3 things you did well today.

- ✍ _____
- ✍ _____
- ✍ _____

Mindfulness Assignment: Good Hugs
Write about your experiences.

_____

_____

_____

_____

_____

_____

_____

_____

_____

_____

_____

_____

_____

_____

_____

I am amazed by how many individuals mess up every new day with yesterday. They insist on bringing into today the failures of yesterday, and in so doing, they pollute a potentially wonderful present.

– Gary Chapman, PhD, "5 Love Languages"

Day 54: _____

Gratitude List
List 5 things you are grateful for.

- _____
- _____
- _____
- _____
- _____

Successes
List 3 things you did well today.

- _____
- _____
- _____

Mindfulness Assignment: Good Hugs
Write about your experiences.

_____

_____

_____

_____

_____

_____

_____

Next Mindfulness Assignment:
Food Providers
Be mindful during one meal a day. As you eat, consider
how the food got to your table. Think of the farmers,
warehouse workers, truck drivers, field workers, cooks,
etc. The work it takes to feed us is tremendous. Honor
the animals and plants giving you life. Be deeply grateful.

Thank you Baron Baptiste, creator of Baptiste Power Yoga and author of several
books such as "40 Days to a Personal Revolution" for this idea.

Day 55: _____

Gratitude List
List 5 things you are grateful for.

- _____
- _____
- _____
- _____
- _____

Successes
List 3 things you did well today.

- _____
- _____
- _____

Mindfulness Assignment: Food Providers
How did it feel to mindfully eat thinking about how your food got to your table? How did it change your experience?

_____
_____
_____
_____
_____
_____
_____
_____
_____
_____
_____
_____
_____
_____
_____
_____
_____

Day 56:

Gratitude List
List 5 things you are grateful for.

-
-
-
-
-

Successes
List 3 things you did well today.

-
-
-

Mindfulness Assignment: Food Providers
Write about your experiences.

If you concentrate on finding what is good in every situation, you will discover that your life will suddenly be filled with gratitude.

–Rabbi Harold Kushner
From the book "The Pocket Therapist" by Therese Borchard

Day 57: _____

Gratitude List
List 5 things you are grateful for.

- _____
- _____
- _____
- _____
- _____

Successes
List 3 things you did well today.

- _____
- _____
- _____

Mindfulness Assignment: Food Providers
Write about your experiences.

_____

_____

_____

_____

_____

_____

_____

_____

Next Mindfulness Assignment:
Nature in Detail
Go outside if you can. (Sitting on a porch is okay.)
Find a natural item in your environment and watch it
for at least a minute. Notice all the small details about
it. Look at it as if you've never seen it before. If
random thoughts occur, let them float off into the
background of your mind. Return your focus to the
item you're watching.

Day 58:

Gratitude List
List 5 things you are grateful for.

- _____
- _____
- _____
- _____
- _____

Successes
List 3 things you did well today.

- _____
- _____
- _____

Mindfulness Assignment: Nature in Detail
How did it go? What details did you notice? Did random thoughts come? Were you able to let them float off or did they steal the show? (It's perfectly natural for thoughts to steal the show. Our practice is to notice when this happens and refocus our attention.)

_____

_____

_____

_____

_____

_____

_____

_____

_____

_____

_____

_____

_____

_____

_____

_____

Day 59: _____

Gratitude List
List 5 things you are grateful for.

- ✍ _____
- ✍ _____
- ✍ _____
- ✍ _____
- ✍ _____

Successes
List 3 things you did well today.

- ✍ _____
- ✍ _____
- ✍ _____

Mindfulness Assignment: Nature in Detail
Write about your experiences.

_____

_____

_____

_____

_____

_____

_____

_____

_____

_____

_____

_____

_____

_____

_____

_____

_____

_____

Day 60: _____

Gratitude List
List 5 things you are grateful for.

- ❧ _____
- ❧ _____
- ❧ _____
- ❧ _____
- ❧ _____

Successes
List 3 things you did well today.

> Check it out! This is day 60! Write this success down! Whoop whoop!

- ❧ _____
- ❧ _____
- ❧ _____

Mindfulness Assignment: Nature in Detail
Write about your experiences.

_____

_____

_____

_____

_____

_____

_____

_____

_____

_____

Reframing reminder
It's hard to change our thinking, but worth the effort. Just be careful to not get down on yourself. Negative thinking is normal! Think of reframing as an alternative, not a replacement, to negative thoughts. Don't try and force negative thoughts to disappear, instead let them take the back seat.

Day 61: _____

Gratitude List
List 5 things you are grateful for.

- ❧ _____
- ❧ _____
- ❧ _____
- ❧ _____
- ❧ _____

Successes
List 3 things you did well today.

- ❧ _____
- ❧ _____
- ❧ _____

Mindfulness Assignment: Nature in Detail
Write about your experiences.

_____

_____

_____

_____

_____

_____

_____

_____

_____

Mega Mindfulness Assignment:
Meditation
Meditate for 5 minutes every day. Sit quietly and listen to your breath, eyes closed or open. You can sit on the floor, up against a wall, or in a chair, or lie on a flat surface; whatever allows you to focus on your breath without falling asleep. Random thoughts will arise and distract you. Don't get angry with yourself. Let them float by and calmly return your focus to your breath.

Day 62:

Gratitude List
List 5 things you are grateful for.

- ❧ _____
- ❧ _____
- ❧ _____
- ❧ _____
- ❧ _____

Successes
List 3 things you did well today.

- ❧ _____
- ❧ _____
- ❧ _____

Mega Mindfulness Assignment: Meditation
How did it go? What was it like listening to your breath? What thoughts came up? Were you able to let them float away? What feelings came up? Were you able to shift focus back to your breath?

_____

_____

_____

_____

_____

_____

_____

_____

If it's too difficult to stay focused on your breath during meditation, see if these techniques help:
- Focus on how your breath registers in a particular body part (e.g. nose, lungs.)
- Count to 4 on the inhale and 4 on the exhale. It's okay to count for the whole meditation.
- If a particular thought or body sensation keeps interrupting, say "thinking" or "feeling" and return to your breath.

Day 63: _____

Gratitude List
List 5 things you are grateful for.

- _____
- _____
- _____
- _____
- _____

Successes
List 3 things you did well today.

- _____
- _____
- _____

Mega Mindfulness Assignment: Meditation
Write about your experiences.

_____

_____

_____

_____

_____

_____   Worrying is a complete
                                           waste of time. The
_____   outcome will be the same
                                           regardless of your
_____   worrying. Practice
                                           visualizing worry thoughts
_____   as words in your mind.
                                           Watch them fade in color
_____   until they're gone.

_____

_____

_____

_____

_____

_____

Day 64:

Gratitude List
List 5 things you are grateful for.

-   _____
-   _____
-   _____
-   _____
-   _____

Successes
List 3 things you did well today.

-   _____
-   _____
-   _____

Mega Mindfulness Assignment: Meditation
Write about your experiences.

_____

_____

_____

_____

_____

_____

_____

_____

✿ Catch the moment!
Whenever a negative thought pops into your head, say to yourself "Hey there Grumpy" and imagine putting ole Grumpy on a cloud and letting him float away. You don't have to let your thoughts beat you up. Just let them drift off.

_____

_____

Day 65: _____

Gratitude List
List 5 things you are grateful for.

- ❧ _____
- ❧ _____
- ❧ _____
- ❧ _____
- ❧ _____

Successes
List 3 things you did well today.

- ❧ _____
- ❧ _____
- ❧ _____

Mega Mindfulness Assignment: Meditation
Write about your experiences.

_____

_____

_____

_____

_____

_____

Next Mindfulness Assignment:
Feet & Toes
At least once a day, put your feet firmly on the floor.
Notice how it feels to press your feet down. Wiggle
your toes. Press your toes into the bottom of your
shoes, or better yet, take off your shoes and feel the
floor. Breathe deep, bring your attention to each toe
individually as you lift and lower them one-by-one.
Be grateful for all your feet and toes do for you.
~ extra assignment ~
Continue daily meditating or repeat one of the exercises
you've done already.

Day 66:

Gratitude List
List 5 things you are grateful for.

-
-
-
-
-

Successes
List 3 things you did well today.

-
-
-

Mindfulness Assignment: Feet & Toes
What was it like focusing on your feet and toes? Were you barefooted? Were you able to stay focused on your feet and toes? Did you do an extra assignment? What did you notice?

Day 67: _____

Gratitude List
List 5 things you are grateful for.

- ❧ _____
- ❧ _____
- ❧ _____
- ❧ _____
- ❧ _____

Successes
List 3 things you did well today.

- ❧ _____
- ❧ _____
- ❧ _____

Mindfulness Assignment: Feet & Toes
Write about your experiences.

_____
_____
_____
_____
_____
_____
_____
_____
_____
_____
_____
_____
_____
_____
_____
_____
_____
_____

Day 68:

Gratitude List
List 5 things you are grateful for.

-
-
-
-
-

Successes
List 3 things you did well today.

-
-
-

Mindfulness Assignment: Feet & Toes
Write about your experiences.

Catch the moment!
As you fold clothes, give thanks to your hands and fingers. Feel the textures of the clothes, smell the aromas, notice the colors. Experience it!

Day 69: _____

Gratitude List
List 5 things you are grateful for.

- _____
- _____
- _____
- _____
- _____

Successes
List 3 things you did well today.

- _____
- _____
- _____

Mindfulness Assignment: Feet & Toes
Write about your experiences.

_____

_____

_____

_____

_____

_____

_____

_____

_____

_____

_____

_____

_____

_____

_____

_____

_____

_____

_____

_____

Day 70:

Gratitude List
List 5 things you are grateful for.

- ❧ _____
- ❧ _____
- ❧ _____
- ❧ _____
- ❧ _____

Successes
List 3 things you did well today.

- ❧ _____
- ❧ _____
- ❧ _____

Mindfulness Assignment: Feet & Toes
Write about your experiences.

_____
_____
_____
_____
_____
_____
_____
_____
_____
_____
_____
_____
_____
_____
_____
_____
_____
_____

Day 71:

Gratitude List
List 5 things you are grateful for.

-   _____
-   _____
-   _____
-   _____
-   _____

Successes
List 3 things you did well today.

-   _____
-   _____
-   _____

Mindfulness Assignment: Feet & Toes
Write about your experiences.

_____

_____

_____

_____

_____

_____

_____

_____

_____

Next Mindfulness Assignment:
Shower/Bath
As you shower or bathe, focus on how great the water feels. Notice how it feels on your head, face, shoulders, back, arms, and legs. If other thoughts intrude, let them float off without judgment and focus on the water.

Day 72: _____

Gratitude List
List 5 things you are grateful for.

- ❧ _____
- ❧ _____
- ❧ _____
- ❧ _____
- ❧ _____

Successes
List 3 things you did well today.

- ❧ _____
- ❧ _____
- ❧ _____

Mindfulness Assignment: Shower/Bath
What was the shower/bath assignment like? How did it feel on your head, face, shoulders, back, arms, and legs? Did other thoughts intrude? Were you able to let them float away and draw your focus back to the water?

_____

_____

_____

_____

_____

_____

_____

_____

_____

_____

_____

_____

_____

_____

_____

_____

Day 73: _____

Gratitude List
List 5 things you are grateful for.

- _____
- _____
- _____
- _____
- _____

Successes
List 3 things you did well today.

- _____
- _____
- _____

Mindfulness Assignment: Shower/Bath
Write about your experiences.

_____
_____
_____
_____
_____
_____
_____
_____
_____
_____
_____
_____
_____
_____
_____
_____
_____
_____
_____

Day 74:

Gratitude List
List 5 things you are grateful for.

- ⇛ _____
- ⇛ _____
- ⇛ _____
- ⇛ _____
- ⇛ _____

Successes
List 3 things you did well today.

- ⇛ _____
- ⇛ _____
- ⇛ _____

Mindfulness Assignment: Shower/Bath
Write about your experiences.

_____

_____

_____

_____

_____

_____

_____

_____

Catch the moment!
When someone compliments you this week, simply say "thank you." Don't follow it up with other words, just simple "thank you". Notice how that feels. What thoughts go through your mind? Do you make excuses like "it was nothing" or "I still need to lose 10 lbs." Do you give yourself enough credit or do you downplay your accomplishments? Consider that responding to someone by downplaying their compliment lowers their self-esteem as much as it lowers yours.

Day 75: _____

Gratitude List
List 5 things you are grateful for.

- ✌ _____
- ✌ _____
- ✌ _____
- ✌ _____
- ✌ _____

Successes
List 3 things you did well today.

- ✌ _____
- ✌ _____
- ✌ _____

Mindfulness Assignment: Shower/Bath
Write about your experiences.

_____

_____

_____

_____

_____

_____

_____

_____

_____

_____

Reframing reminder
We can be so hard on ourselves when it comes to our bodies. Can you reframe your thoughts in this area? Instead of focusing on what your body lacks, can you focus on what it provides?

Think of how your body assists you in daily life, moving you through your day.

Day 76:

Gratitude List
List 5 things you are grateful for.

- _____
- _____
- _____
- _____
- _____

Successes
List 3 things you did well today.

- _____
- _____
- _____

Mindfulness Assignment: Shower/Bath
Write about your experiences.

_____
_____
_____
_____
_____
_____
_____
_____
_____
_____
_____
_____
_____
_____
_____
_____
_____
_____

Day 77: _____

Gratitude List
List 5 things you are grateful for.

- _____
- _____
- _____
- _____
- _____

Successes
List 3 things you did well today.

- _____
- _____
- _____

Mindfulness Assignment: Shower/Bath
Write about your experiences.

_____

_____

_____

_____

_____

_____

_____

Next Mindfulness Assignment:
Relationship Presence

Every day, give your loved ones full attention. Put down the computer, stop texting, turn off the TV -- whatever you need to do to be fully present with them. Focus on their words and be grateful for your relationships.

~ extra assignment ~

Throughout the day, try to not anticipate what's going to happen next, but instead be open to whatever happens.

Day 78:

Gratitude List
List 5 things you are grateful for.

- _____
- _____
- _____
- _____
- _____

Successes
List 3 things you did well today.

- _____
- _____
- _____

Mindfulness Assignments: Relationship Presence
Were you able to give a loved one your full attention today? What was it like? What helped or hindered you in being fully present? Did you do the extra assignment and try not to anticipate what's going to happen, but be open? How did it go?

_____

_____

_____

_____

_____

_____

_____

_____

_____

_____

_____

_____

_____

_____

_____

_____

Day 79: _____

Gratitude List
List 5 things you are grateful for.

- _____
- _____
- _____
- _____
- _____

Successes
List 3 things you did well today.

- _____
- _____
- _____

Mindfulness Assignment: Relationship Presence
Write about your experiences.

_____

_____

_____

_____

_____

_____

_____

_____

_____

_____

_____

_____

When I sit with my wife and give her twenty minutes of my undivided attention and she does the same for me, we are giving each other twenty minutes of life. We will never have those twenty minutes again; we are giving our lives to each other.

– Gary Chapman, "5 Love Languages"

_____

_____

Day 80:

Gratitude List
List 5 things you are grateful for.

- ❧ _____
- ❧ _____
- ❧ _____
- ❧ _____
- ❧ _____

Successes
List 3 things you did well today.

- ❧ _____
- ❧ _____
- ❧ _____

Mindfulness Assignment: Relationship Presence
Write about your experiences.

_____

_____

_____

_____

_____

_____

_____

_____

_____

_____

_____

_____

_____

_____

_____

_____

_____

Day 81: _____

Gratitude List
List 5 things you are grateful for.

- _____
- _____
- _____
- _____
- _____

Successes
List 3 things you did well today.

- _____
- _____
- _____

Mindfulness Assignment: Relationship Presence
Write about your experiences.

_____

_____

_____

_____

_____

_____

_____

_____

_____

_____

_____

_____

_____

_____

_____

_____

Day 82:

Gratitude List
List 5 things you are grateful for.

- ❧ _____
- ❧ _____
- ❧ _____
- ❧ _____
- ❧ _____

Successes
List 3 things you did well today.

- ❧ _____
- ❧ _____
- ❧ _____

Mindfulness Assignment: Relationship Presence
Write about your experiences.

_____

_____

_____

_____

_____

_____

_____

_____

_____

Next Mindfulness Assignment:
Color Red
Every time you find yourself being too much in your
head, look around to see items that are the color red. If
your mind starts to wander again, focus on finding red.
Do this in your car, in meetings, at home, etc. This is a
useful tool to use wherever and whenever you find
yourself too wrapped up in thought.

Day 83: _____

Gratitude List
List 5 things you are grateful for.

- _____
- _____
- _____
- _____
- _____

Successes
List 3 things you did well today.

- _____
- _____
- _____

Mindfulness Assignment: Color Red
Were you able to catch yourself being too much in your head? Could you stop and focus on finding red? What thoughts kept coming back?

_____

_____

_____

_____

_____

_____

_____

_____

_____

_____

_____

_____

_____

_____

_____

_____

_____

Day 84:

Gratitude List
List 5 things you are grateful for.

- ❧ _____
- ❧ _____
- ❧ _____
- ❧ _____
- ❧ _____

Successes
List 3 things you did well today.

- ❧ _____
- ❧ _____
- ❧ _____

Mindfulness Assignment: Color Red
Write about your experiences.

_____

_____

_____

_____

_____

_____

_____

_____

_____

_____

_____

_____

_____

_____

_____

_____

_____

Day 85: _____

Gratitude List
List 5 things you are grateful for.

- ❦ _____
- ❦ _____
- ❦ _____
- ❦ _____
- ❦ _____

Successes
List 3 things you did well today.

- ❦ _____
- ❦ _____
- ❦ _____

Mindfulness Assignment: Color Red
Write about your experiences.

_____

_____

_____

_____

_____

_____

_____

_____

_____

_____

_____

_____

Catch the moment!
As you fold clothes, give thanks to the people in your life. As you hold a piece of clothing belonging to someone else, think of them and how you feel about them.

Day 86:

Gratitude List
List 5 things you are grateful for.

- _____
- _____
- _____
- _____
- _____

Successes
List 3 things you did well today.

- _____
- _____
- _____

Mindfulness Assignment: Color Red
Write about your experiences.

_____
_____
_____
_____
_____
_____
_____
_____
_____
_____
_____
_____
_____
_____
_____
_____
_____
_____
_____

Day 87: _____

Gratitude List
List 5 things you are grateful for.

- 🙎 _____
- 🙎 _____
- 🙎 _____
- 🙎 _____
- 🙎 _____

Successes
List 3 things you did well today.

- 🙎 _____
- 🙎 _____
- 🙎 _____

Mindfulness Assignment: Color Red
Write about your experiences.

_____

_____

_____

_____

_____

_____

_____

Next Mindfulness Assignment:
Breath
At least once a day, put your hand on your neck.
Notice how warm your skin is, how your blood pulses,
how soft the skin is under your fingers. Breathe in and
out for at least 2 minutes. Be grateful you can breathe,
and know your breath is always here for you to help
you come back to the present.
~ extra assignment ~
Daily meditation focusing on your breath is a wonderful
complement to this assignment.

Day 88: _____

Gratitude List
List 5 things you are grateful for.

-   _____
-   _____
-   _____
-   _____
-   _____

Successes
List 3 things you did well today.

-   _____
-   _____
-   _____

Mindfulness Assignment: Breath
Did you remember to put your hand on your neck? How did the warmth feel? Were you able to focus on your breathing for 2 minutes? Express your gratitude for your breath? Did you do the meditation too? How did that go?

_____

_____

_____

_____

_____

_____

_____

_____

_____

_____

_____

_____

_____

_____

_____

Day 89: _____

Gratitude List
List 5 things you are grateful for.

- ❧ _____
- ❧ _____
- ❧ _____
- ❧ _____
- ❧ _____

Successes
List 3 things you did well today.

- ❧ _____
- ❧ _____
- ❧ _____

Mindfulness Assignment: Breath
Write about your experiences.

_____
_____
_____
_____
_____
_____
_____
_____
_____
_____
_____
_____
_____
_____
_____
_____
_____
_____
_____

Day 90: _____

Gratitude List
List 5 things you are grateful for.

- ❧ _____
- ❧ _____
- ❧ _____
- ❧ _____
- ❧ _____

Successes
List 3 things you did well today.

{ Three months!
Great work! }

- ❧ _____
- ❧ _____
- ❧ _____

Mindfulness Assignment: Breath
Write about your experiences.

_____

_____

_____

_____

_____

_____

_____

_____

_____

✿

_____

If you're breathing, you're alive and your body is working... bringing oxygen into the body, which gives you energy, help digest your food, cleans out toxins, fuels muscles, and keeps the heart pumping... Every breath is a gift, and the awareness of breathing can give rise to the healing nature of gratitude.

– Drs. Elisha Goldstein and Bob Stahl, "MBSR Every Day: Daily Practices from the Heart of Mindfulness-Based Stress Reduction"

Day 91: _____

Gratitude List
List 5 things you are grateful for.

- _____
- _____
- _____
- _____
- _____

Successes
List 3 things you did well today.

- _____
- _____
- _____

Mindfulness Assignment: Breath
Write about your experiences.

_____
_____
_____
_____
_____
_____
_____
_____
_____
_____
_____
_____
_____
_____
_____
_____
_____
_____

Day 92: _____

Gratitude List
List 5 things you are grateful for.

- _____
- _____
- _____
- _____
- _____

Successes
List 3 things you did well today.

- _____
- _____
- _____

Mindfulness Assignment: Breath
Write about your experiences.

_____

_____

_____

_____

_____

_____

_____

_____

_____

Next Mindfulness Assignment:
Drop Judgment
At least once a day, pick one person and really see them (it can be a stranger or someone you know.) Notice your thoughts as you size them up or judge them. Then choose to see them again without judgment. Drop what you think you know about them and consider you know very little, if anything, about them. Look at them with new eyes.

Day 93: _____

Gratitude List
List 5 things you are grateful for.

- _____
- _____
- _____
- _____
- _____

Successes
List 3 things you did well today.

- _____
- _____
- _____

Mindfulness Assignment: Drop Judgment
Write about your experiences.

_____

_____

_____

_____

_____

_____

_____

_____

_____

_____

_____

_____

_____

_____

_____

_____

_____

_____

_____

Day 94:

Gratitude List
List 5 things you are grateful for.

-
-
-
-
-

Successes
List 3 things you did well today.

-
-
-

Mindfulness Assignment: Drop Judgment
How did it go? What were your preconceived notions/judgments?
Were you able to drop those and look again? What was that like?

You've heard the saying "do what you love," right? This can be tough – life circumstances can get in the way of fulfilling our dreams. Or maybe what we need is a shift in perspective.

Instead, could you learn to "love what you do?" Rather than focusing on what you're not doing, see a new way to love the path you're on. You've seen how being mindful of ordinary things can bring more awareness and gratitude. Take these tools out into the world and bring mindfulness to other activities and reframe your thoughts about your situation. Look for what you can treasure. See how you have the opportunity to live your values as you do the "daily grind."

Day 95: _____

Gratitude List
List 5 things you are grateful for.

- _____
- _____
- _____
- _____
- _____

Successes
List 3 things you did well today.

- _____
- _____
- _____

Mindfulness Assignment: Drop Judgment
Write about your experiences.

_____

_____

_____

_____

_____

_____

_____

_____

_____

_____

_____

_____

_____

_____

_____

_____

_____

_____

Day 96:

Gratitude List
List 5 things you are grateful for.

- _____
- _____
- _____
- _____
- _____

Successes
List 3 things you did well today.

- _____
- _____
- _____

Mindfulness Assignment: Drop Judgment
Write about your experiences.

_____
_____
_____
_____
_____
_____
_____
_____
_____
_____
_____
_____
_____

Make a moment!
Take time this week to do something enjoyable, something just for you.

Day 97: _____

Gratitude List
List 5 things you are grateful for.

- _____
- _____
- _____
- _____
- _____

Successes
List 3 things you did well today.

- _____
- _____
- _____

Mindfulness Assignment: Drop Judgment
Write about your experiences.

_____

_____

_____

_____

_____

_____

_____

_____

_____

_____

_____

Next Mindfulness Assignment:
Good Morning
Don't just hop out of bed in the morning. Take a
moment to listen to your breath, feel the mattress and
sheets, birds chirping, etc. Be thankful you are alive.

Day 98: _____

Gratitude List
List 5 things you are grateful for.

- _____
- _____
- _____
- _____
- _____

Successes
List 3 things you did well today.

- _____
- _____
- _____

Mindfulness Assignments: Good Morning
What was morning like? What did you hear around you? Did you listen to your breath or feel the mattress and sheets? Express your gratitude that you're alive?

_____

_____

_____

_____

_____

✿ Reframing reminder
Mornings can be difficult. When I'm going through a depression episode, it's difficult to wake up knowing I'll still be depressed. Instead of getting dragged down into the pit, I reframe my thoughts; focus on the depressive thoughts as merely symptoms of an illness. I don't assign meaning or get attached to them.

We can come up with many alternatives to our thoughts. Ask yourself "is this thought helpful?" If it is, go with it. If not, chuck it and come up with another thought. There is so much power in knowing you can choose.

Day 99: _____

Gratitude List
List 5 things you are grateful for.

- ∾ _____
- ∾ _____
- ∾ _____
- ∾ _____
- ∾ _____

Successes
List 3 things you did well today.

- ∾ _____
- ∾ _____
- ∾ _____

Mindfulness Assignments: Good Morning
Write about your experiences.

_____

_____

_____

_____

_____

_____

_____

_____

_____

_____

_____

_____

_____

_____

_____

_____

_____

_____

Day 100:

Gratitude List
List 5 things you are grateful for.

 _____
 _____
 _____
 _____
 _____

Successes
List 3 things you did well today.

 _____
 _____
 _____

Mindfulness Assignments: Good Morning
Write about your experiences.

_____
_____
_____
_____
_____
_____
_____
_____
_____
_____
_____
_____
_____
_____
_____
_____
_____

You have completed
100 days of mindfulness!

Congratulations! You did it! I hope this
journaling adventure has been helpful
to you.

*Be sure to check out the Appendix
for ideas for growing your
mindfulness practice.*

*I wish you the very best of everything
in life. My spirit sees and honors
your spirit.*

NAMASTE

Reflection
What were your favorite mindfulness activities? Have
you noticed any change in your ability to calm your
mind and focus? How does that feel?

Which activities did not do much for you? Could
those activities provide you with a different
experience next time?

Appendix

Growing Your Mindfulness Practice

So where do you go from here? Here are some options to consider.

Books and workbooks –Below are some authors I have enjoyed and been influenced by on my mindfulness journey:

- o Brene Brown, PhD
- o Thich Nhat Hanh
- o Martin Seligman
- o Russ Harris
- o Baron Baptiste
- o Elisha Goldstein, PhD, and Bob Stahl, PhD
- o Kamini Desai
- o Therese Borchard

Yoga – Thousands of years ago, the practice of yoga was created as a way to prepare the mind for meditation. It's sometimes referred to as a "moving meditation." Yoga is amazing, and I have personally experienced a life transformation from the practice. I can't recommend yoga highly enough as a way to get out of your head and into your body. Below are some common venues where yoga classes can be found:

- o Colleges often have beginner yoga classes available to the community for low cost
- o Most gyms have yoga classes on their schedules
- o Yoga studios usually have classes every day
- o Hospitals often have community wellness programs
- o The free website Meetup (www.meetup.com) will help you find yoga classes in your area

Meditation – There is a wide variety of meditation styles out there to try. If you're unfamiliar with meditation, I suggest guided meditation where a voice leads you. The availability of guided meditation is tremendous:

- o Smartphone apps such as Headspace, Calm, Buddify, Omvana and the Mindfulness App.
- o YouTube videos
- o iTunes and Amazon Music
- o CDs and tapes for purchase on Amazon
- o The free website Meetup (www.meetup.com) will help you find meditation sessions in your area
- o Yoga studios often have meditation classes too
- o Unity Church (www.unity.org) and Unitarian Universalist Church (www.uua.org)
- o Buddhist Centers (some meditation sessions can last 1-2 hours, so inquire with them about their schedule before you go.)

More Gratitude Ideas

Recalling activities or events from the day can be a source of gratitude. It's just a matter of wording them in a grateful way.

For example, you went to a concert you really enjoyed. You could write, "I am grateful I have the financial means to attend concerts" or "I am grateful for music; it lifts my spirits."

I use my gratitude section to express my gratitude for the things I get to experience, which also serves as a historical record of my life.

Other ideas:

- Family and friends who support you. List each person individually and what specifically you're grateful for. It could be something they did today.
- Sunny day, warm day, rainy day
- Ability to breathe
- Pets, children, and loved ones showing you they love you. Again, list them individually and what specifically you love about them.
- Ability to move, walk, exercise, etc.
- Ability to eat, burp, pass gas, even poop!
- Eating yummy food.
- Having a good boss.
- Having coworkers.
- Encountering nice smells.
- Clean water, air conditioning, and heat.
- Having clothes to wear.
- Having electronics (TV, cell phone, computer, tablet, etc.)
- Music, being able to hear.
- The sounds of nature.
- Having shelter.
- Being able to see colors.
- Having electricity, the Internet.
- Seeing art.
- Being able to read a book.
- Friends and family.
- Hearing laughter.
- Baby animals always make me smile.
- It can be a fun daily exercise to name one thing you like about a person in your life. You may learn you appreciate much more about them than you realize.

More Successes

Anytime you think of something you did today as not special or too mundane to be a success, shift your thinking. Little accomplishments are still accomplishments.

- o Going to work when you don't feel well
- o Making dinner
- o Eating healthy
- o Sleeping well
- o Getting chores done
- o Getting bills paid
- o Telling someone you love them
- o Enjoying something without being distracted by thoughts

Value-Based Living – Additional Guidance

The best way I can think of to give more guidance is to provide my own example of using my chosen values to shift my perspective (and hence my mood.)

My values are compassion, generosity, and connection. I remind myself of these values every morning and often think of them during the day. I use these values as guideposts for how I think and react. Some examples of how I use them:

- When I'm in a situation that feels off, my values help me know what to do. I ask myself "is this situation in keeping with my values? Can I change the situation with my actions? Do I need to excuse myself?"

- Gossip is a problem area for me. When I catch myself being part of gossip, I mentally ask "Am I being compassionate or generous? Is this fostering connection with others?"

- Sometimes my depression makes me want to isolate. I use my value of connection to push myself to go out and be with others (because I know that I really do want connection, it's just my disease getting in the way.)

- For a long time, I was really down on my job. I work for a health insurance company, and it's a big company with lots of cubicles. It's essentially Corporate America. I felt my job wasn't altruistic enough. I wanted to help people. I use my values at work and it has improved my interactions with coworkers. But I started to realize I could take my values-based living to a higher level. Instead of just applying my values to the situation of the moment, I started actively looking for opportunities to exercise my generosity and compassion, to help my coworkers. This led to me becoming a voice for people with mental illness, as well as fighting for the rights of my LGBT coworkers.

Using values to guide my actions helps my anxiety and depression in three ways:

1. It reduces that nagging feeling something is wrong. I believe this feeling comes from disconnect between our values and how we're living our lives. Sometimes we are conscious of this disconnect, but often we aren't and instead know it subconsciously. Either way, the result is unease, which turns into anxiety, and then into depression.

2. Instead of obsessing and stressing over decisions, I bounce the decision against my values to help me decide faster. This way I spend less time under stress. Because I used my values to make my decision, I experience less regret.

3. The many mundane things in my life that used to depress me now have purpose.

It's your turn! Below are some values to get you started:

Accuracy	Faith	Patriotism
Achievement	Family	Perfection
Belonging	Fidelity	Productivity
Cheerfulness	Fitness	Prudence
Commitment	Forgiveness	Quality
Compassion	Freedom	Responsibility
Competitiveness	Fun	Results-
Consistency	Generosity	Oriented
Control	Grace	Safety and
Courage	Growth	Security
Creativity	Hard Work	Self-
Curiosity	Helping Others	Actualization
Dependability	Humility	Self-Control
Devotion	Intellect	Self-Reliance
Diligence	Intelligence	Serenity
Discipline	Justice	Spontaneity
Discretion	Leaving a Legacy	Tolerance
Diversity	Love	Trustworthiness
Education	Loyalty	Truth-Seeking
Efficiency	Making a Difference	Uniqueness
Empathy	Mastery	Usefulness
Enthusiasm	Openness	Vitality
Excellence	Order	
Exploration	Originality	

About the Author

Tracey Moore Lukkarila has worked in the health insurance industry for nearly two decades in a variety of Information Technology and Public Policy roles. She holds a bachelor's degree in Business Administration from the University of North Florida and a masters-level certificate in Public Health from the University of Florida. She is a registered yoga teacher (RYT-200).

Tracey strives to live out her personal values of compassion, generosity, connectedness, and education. She serves as the chair of her employer's lesbian, gay, bisexual, and transgender (LGBT) group, advocating for LGBT rights in the workplace and statewide. Tracey is very passionate about animals and volunteers for the animal shelter community. She loves yoga and teaches the Baptiste Power Yoga methodology in her community. As a lifelong sufferer of anxiety and depression, she aims to bring her professional and personal experiences together to advocate for mental health and to help others who struggle.

Tracey also enjoys arts and crafts, music, film, traveling, hiking, camping, and spending time with friends. She lives with her husband Troy and their six cats and dog in Florida.

Visit her blog at www.traceylukkarila.com.